THIS BOOK BELONGS TO

_____

For whatever things were written before were written for our learning, that we through the patience and comfort of the Scriptures might have hope.

Romans 15:4

Copyright © 2025 by Shepherds
Shepherds, Made in USA. ALL rights reserved

visit us on the web!
GODSSHEPHERDS.COM

Shepherds children's books
support the First Amendment and celebrates
the right to read.

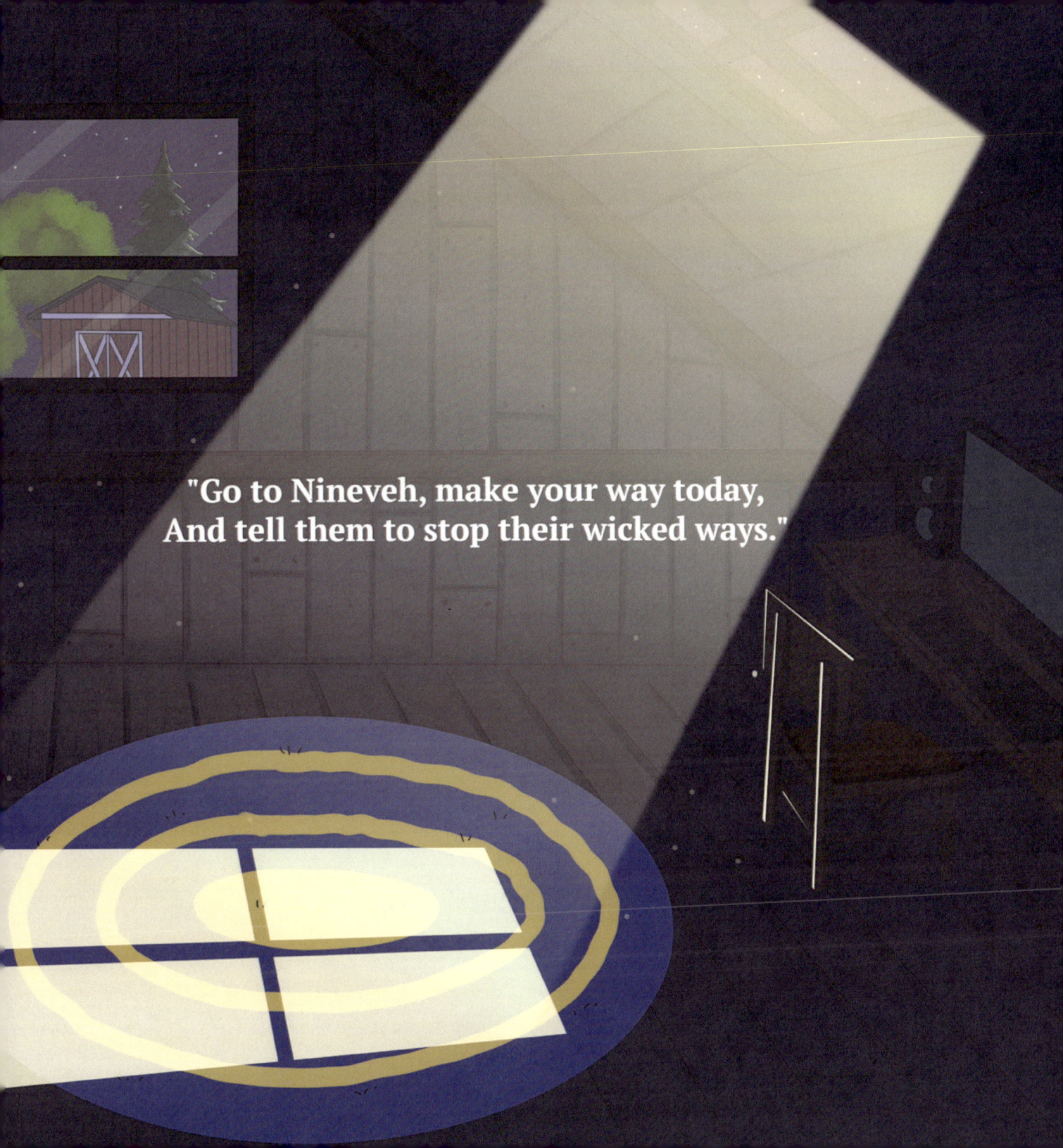
"Go to Nineveh, make your way today,
And tell them to stop their wicked ways."

He found a boat and climbed aboard,
Hoping to escape the Lord.

Reluctantly, they tossed him out,
And the sea grew calm, without a doubt.

But Jonah sank into the deep,
Where a giant fish began to creep.
Swallowed whole, in the belly he stayed,
For three long nights and three long days.

God spoke to the fish, "Spit Jonah out."
Onto dry land, Jonah went, without a doubt.

Again, God spoke to Jonah, and he obeyed what was heard.
And set off to Nineveh to share God's word.

But Jonah, filled with confusion inside,
Asked, "Why show mercy?
They should have been denied!"

Now, in a big fuss, Jonah sat himself down.
Why God? Why did you forgive that town?

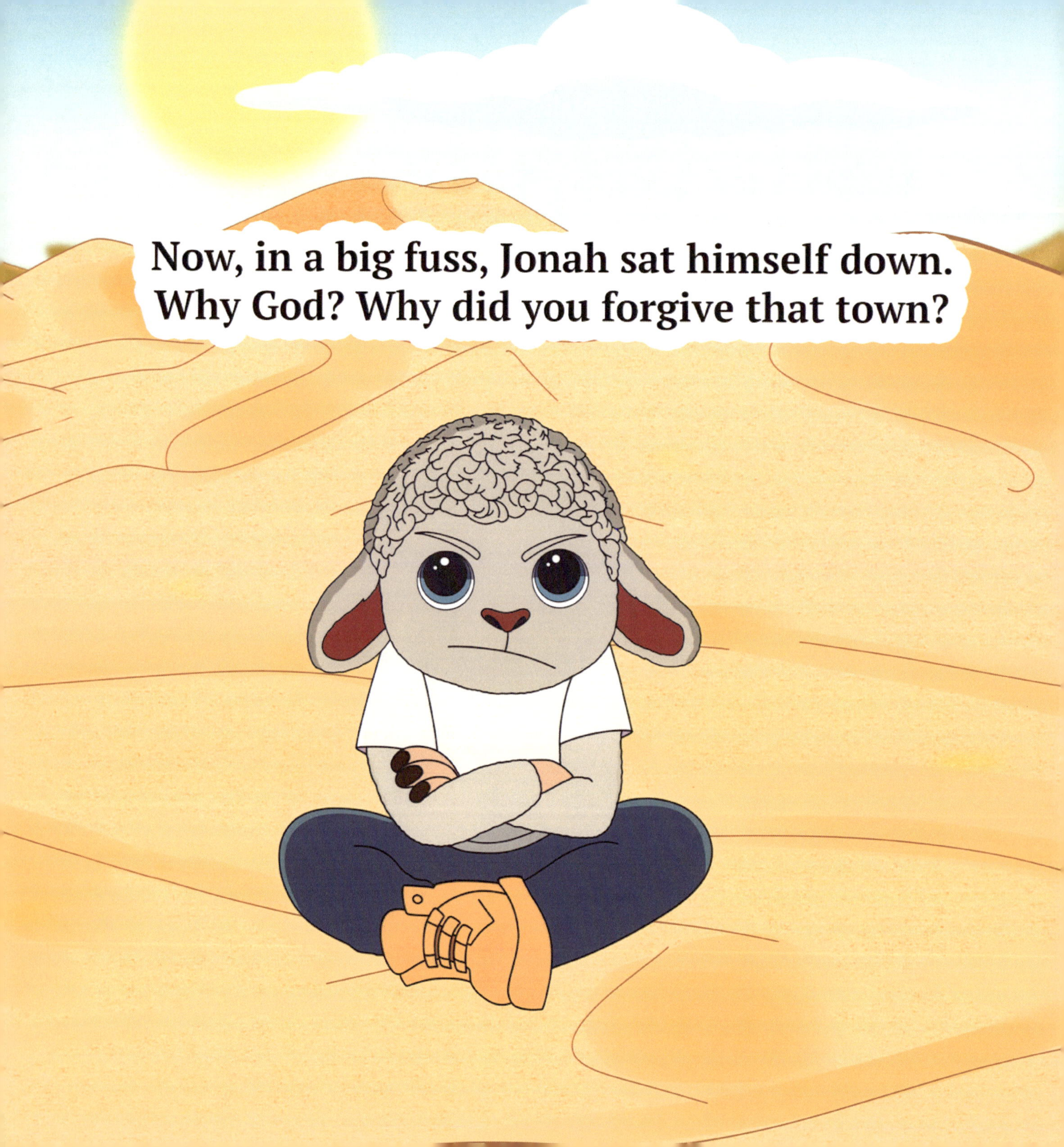

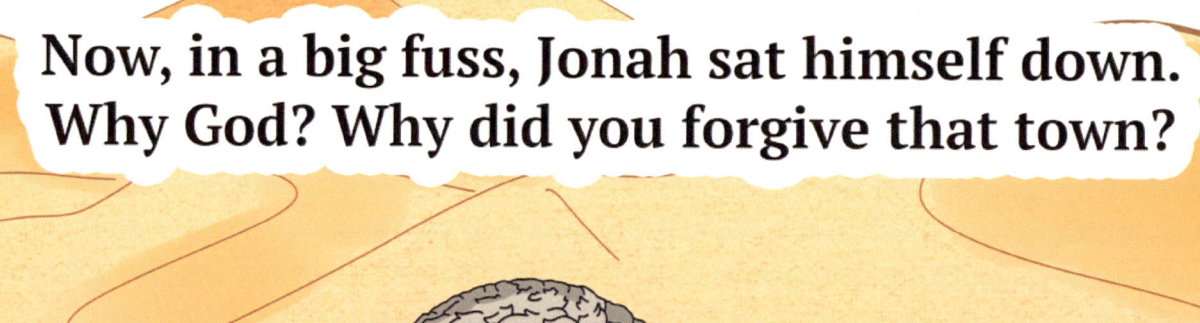

God then provided a plant
To give Jonah some shade.
He was now more comfortable
In the place where he lay.

Soon after, God sent a worm to chew up the plant.
Jonah fumed in the scorching heat and started to rant.
God gently spoke, why are you angry? Why do you rant?
Might I add, you did not tend or grow this plant.

SHEP✝HERDS

- A person who herds, tends, and guards sheep. A person who protects, guides, or watches over a person or group of people.

JONAH AND THE GREAT FISH

By: Marcus A. Smith

www.ingramcontent.com/pod-product-compliance
Lightning Source LLC
LaVergne TN
LVRC091352060526
838201LV00019B/289